Committing Suicide
for Geniuses

By I. M. Cryingforhelp

www.justforgeniuses.com

DISCLAIMER: The book is a work of parody. Nothing in this book is meant to imply any facts about any actual persons or entities.

All rights reserved. No part of this publication may be reproduced, distributed, or transmitted in any form or by any means, including photocopying, recording, or other electronic or mechanical methods, without the prior written permission of the publisher.

Copyright © 2014 by Westlake Gavin Publishers LLC

Just for Geniuses, For Geniuses, and accompanying logos are trademarks of Westlake Gavin Publishers LLC and may not be used without written permission. All other trademarks are the property of their respective owners. Westlake Gavin Publishers LLC, is not associated with any other product or service mentioned in this book.

HUMANS OF MIRTH COLLECTION   TGGT1001

Library of *Con*-gress Cataloging-in-Publication Data

Committing Suicide for Geniuses / by I. M. Cryingforhelp
p. cm.
ISBN 978-1-63231-999-9
1. Cryingforhelp, I. M.   2. Parody, imitations, etc.   I. Title.

First Edition

10 9 8 7 6 5 4 3 2 1

Inside...

The most effective methods to end it all. Not for the squeamish.

How to make everyone feel really guilty for not being nicer to you when they still had the chance.

How to have fun as a paraplegic for the rest of your life (in case your suicide attempt fails.)

How to write an effective suicide note. Remember: you don't get to clarify... you don't get to explain. It's game over. For real. Forever.

Did you know that one warning sign of suicide is talking about wanting to die?

If you or someone you know may be at risk for suicide, please call the **National Suicide Prevention Lifeline** at **800-273-8255** night or day. The call is **free** and is **completely confidential**.

To learn more warning signs and how you can help prevent suicide, please visit **www.SuicidePreventionLifeline.org**.

(All profits from the sale of this book will be donated by the author to charities supporting suicide prevention, education and research.)

Committing Suicide *for Geniuses*

Did you know that one warning sign of suicide is talking about wanting to die?

If you or someone you know may be at risk for suicide, please call the **National Suicide Prevention Lifeline** at **800-273-8255** night or day. The call is **free** and is **completely confidential**.

To learn more warning signs and how you can help prevent suicide, please visit **www.SuicidePreventionLifeline.org**.

(All profits from the sale of this book will be donated by the author to charities supporting suicide prevention, education and research.)

Read enough? Turn to page 104.

Committing Suicide *for Geniuses*

Did you know that one warning sign of suicide is talking about wanting to die?

If you or someone you know may be at risk for suicide, please call the **National Suicide Prevention Lifeline** at **800-273-8255** night or day. The call is **free** and is **completely confidential**.

To learn more warning signs and how you can help prevent suicide, please visit **www.SuicidePreventionLifeline.org**.

(All profits from the sale of this book will be donated by the author to charities supporting suicide prevention, education and research.)

Read enough? Turn to page 104.

Committing Suicide *for Geniuses*

Did you know that one warning sign of suicide is talking about wanting to die?

If you or someone you know may be at risk for suicide, please call the **National Suicide Prevention Lifeline** at **800-273-8255** night or day. The call is **free** and is **completely confidential**.

To learn more warning signs and how you can help prevent suicide, please visit **www.SuicidePreventionLifeline.org**.

(All profits from the sale of this book will be donated by the author to charities supporting suicide prevention, education and research.)

Read enough? Turn to page 104.

Committing Suicide *for Geniuses*

Did you know that one warning sign of suicide is talking about wanting to die?

If you or someone you know may be at risk for suicide, please call the **National Suicide Prevention Lifeline** at **800-273-8255** night or day. The call is **free** and is **completely confidential**.

To learn more warning signs and how you can help prevent suicide, please visit **www.SuicidePreventionLifeline.org**.

(All profits from the sale of this book will be donated by the author to charities supporting suicide prevention, education and research.)

Read enough? Turn to page 104.

Committing Suicide *for Geniuses*

Did you know that one warning sign of suicide is talking about wanting to die?

If you or someone you know may be at risk for suicide, please call the **National Suicide Prevention Lifeline** at **800-273-8255** night or day. The call is **free** and is **completely confidential**.

To learn more warning signs and how you can help prevent suicide, please visit **www.SuicidePreventionLifeline.org**.

(All profits from the sale of this book will be donated by the author to charities supporting suicide prevention, education and research.)

Read enough? Turn to page 104.

Committing Suicide *for Geniuses*

Did you know that one warning sign of suicide is talking about wanting to die?

If you or someone you know may be at risk for suicide, please call the **National Suicide Prevention Lifeline** at **800-273-8255** night or day. The call is **free** and is **completely confidential**.

To learn more warning signs and how you can help prevent suicide, please visit **www.SuicidePreventionLifeline.org**.

(All profits from the sale of this book will be donated by the author to charities supporting suicide prevention, education and research.)

Read enough? Turn to page 104.

Committing Suicide *for Geniuses*

Did you know that one warning sign of suicide is talking about wanting to die?

If you or someone you know may be at risk for suicide, please call the **National Suicide Prevention Lifeline** at **800-273-8255** night or day. The call is **free** and is **completely confidential**.

To learn more warning signs and how you can help prevent suicide, please visit **www.SuicidePreventionLifeline.org**.

(All profits from the sale of this book will be donated by the author to charities supporting suicide prevention, education and research.)

Read enough? Turn to page 104.

Committing Suicide *for Geniuses*

Committing Suicide *for Geniuses*

Did you know that one warning sign of suicide is talking about wanting to die?

If you or someone you know may be at risk for suicide, please call the **National Suicide Prevention Lifeline** at **800-273-8255** night or day. The call is **free** and is **completely confidential**.

To learn more warning signs and how you can help prevent suicide, please visit **www.SuicidePreventionLifeline.org**.

(All profits from the sale of this book will be donated by the author to charities supporting suicide prevention, education and research.)

Read enough? Turn to page 104.

Committing Suicide *for Geniuses*

Did you know that one warning sign of suicide is talking about wanting to die?

If you or someone you know may be at risk for suicide, please call the **National Suicide Prevention Lifeline** at **800-273-8255** night or day. The call is **free** and is **completely confidential**.

To learn more warning signs and how you can help prevent suicide, please visit **www.SuicidePreventionLifeline.org**.

(All profits from the sale of this book will be donated by the author to charities supporting suicide prevention, education and research.)

Read enough? Turn to page 104.

Did you know that one warning sign of suicide is talking about wanting to die?

If you or someone you know may be at risk for suicide, please call the **National Suicide Prevention Lifeline** at **800-273-8255** night or day. The call is **free** and is **completely confidential**.

To learn more warning signs and how you can help prevent suicide, please visit **www.SuicidePreventionLifeline.org**.

(All profits from the sale of this book will be donated by the author to charities supporting suicide prevention, education and research.)

Read enough? Turn to page 104.

Committing Suicide *for Geniuses*

Did you know that one warning sign of suicide is talking about wanting to die?

If you or someone you know may be at risk for suicide, please call the **National Suicide Prevention Lifeline** at **800-273-8255** night or day. The call is **free** and is **completely confidential**.

To learn more warning signs and how you can help prevent suicide, please visit **www.SuicidePreventionLifeline.org**.

(All profits from the sale of this book will be donated by the author to charities supporting suicide prevention, education and research.)

Read enough? Turn to page 104.

Did you know that one warning sign of suicide is talking about wanting to die?

If you or someone you know may be at risk for suicide, please call the **National Suicide Prevention Lifeline** at **800-273-8255** night or day. The call is **free** and is **completely confidential**.

To learn more warning signs and how you can help prevent suicide, please visit **www.SuicidePreventionLifeline.org**.

(All profits from the sale of this book will be donated by the author to charities supporting suicide prevention, education and research.)

Read enough? Turn to page 104.

Committing Suicide *for Geniuses*

Committing Suicide *for Geniuses*

Did you know that one warning sign of suicide is talking about wanting to die?

If you or someone you know may be at risk for suicide, please call the **National Suicide Prevention Lifeline** at **800-273-8255** night or day. The call is **free** and is **completely confidential**.

To learn more warning signs and how you can help prevent suicide, please visit **www.SuicidePreventionLifeline.org**.

(All profits from the sale of this book will be donated by the author to charities supporting suicide prevention, education and research.)

Read enough? Turn to page 104.

Did you know that one warning sign of suicide is talking about wanting to die?

If you or someone you know may be at risk for suicide, please call the **National Suicide Prevention Lifeline** at **800-273-8255** night or day. The call is **free** and is **completely confidential**.

To learn more warning signs and how you can help prevent suicide, please visit **www.SuicidePreventionLifeline.org**.

(All profits from the sale of this book will be donated by the author to charities supporting suicide prevention, education and research.)

Read enough? Turn to page 104.

Committing Suicide *for Geniuses*

Did you know that one warning sign of suicide is talking about wanting to die?

If you or someone you know may be at risk for suicide, please call the **National Suicide Prevention Lifeline** at **800-273-8255** night or day. The call is **free** and is **completely confidential**.

To learn more warning signs and how you can help prevent suicide, please visit **www.SuicidePreventionLifeline.org**.

(All profits from the sale of this book will be donated by the author to charities supporting suicide prevention, education and research.)

Read enough? Turn to page 104.

Committing Suicide *for Geniuses*

_____
_____
_____
_____
_____
_____
_____
_____
_____
_____
_____
_____
_____
_____
_____
_____
_____
_____
_____
_____
_____
_____
_____
_____

Did you know that one warning sign of suicide is talking about wanting to die?

If you or someone you know may be at risk for suicide, please call the **National Suicide Prevention Lifeline** at **800-273-8255** night or day. The call is **free** and is **completely confidential**.

To learn more warning signs and how you can help prevent suicide, please visit **www.SuicidePreventionLifeline.org**.

(All profits from the sale of this book will be donated by the author to charities supporting suicide prevention, education and research.)

Read enough? Turn to page 104.

Did you know that one warning sign of suicide is talking about wanting to die?

If you or someone you know may be at risk for suicide, please call the **National Suicide Prevention Lifeline** at **800-273-8255** night or day. The call is **free** and is **completely confidential**.

To learn more warning signs and how you can help prevent suicide, please visit **www.SuicidePreventionLifeline.org**.

(All profits from the sale of this book will be donated by the author to charities supporting suicide prevention, education and research.)

Read enough? Turn to page 104.

Committing Suicide *for Geniuses*

Did you know that one warning sign of suicide is talking about wanting to die?

If you or someone you know may be at risk for suicide, please call the **National Suicide Prevention Lifeline** at **800-273-8255** night or day. The call is **free** and is **completely confidential**.

To learn more warning signs and how you can help prevent suicide, please visit **www.SuicidePreventionLifeline.org**.

(All profits from the sale of this book will be donated by the author to charities supporting suicide prevention, education and research.)

Read enough? Turn to page 104.

Did you know that one warning sign of suicide is talking about wanting to die?

If you or someone you know may be at risk for suicide, please call the **National Suicide Prevention Lifeline** at **800-273-8255** night or day. The call is **free** and is **completely confidential**.

To learn more warning signs and how you can help prevent suicide, please visit **www.SuicidePreventionLifeline.org**.

(All profits from the sale of this book will be donated by the author to charities supporting suicide prevention, education and research.)

Read enough? Turn to page 104.

Did you know that one warning sign of suicide is talking about wanting to die?

If you or someone you know may be at risk for suicide, please call the **National Suicide Prevention Lifeline** at **800-273-8255** night or day. The call is **free** and is **completely confidential**.

To learn more warning signs and how you can help prevent suicide, please visit **www.SuicidePreventionLifeline.org**.

(All profits from the sale of this book will be donated by the author to charities supporting suicide prevention, education and research.)

Read enough? Turn to page 104.

Committing Suicide *for Geniuses*

Committing Suicide *for Geniuses*

Did you know that one warning sign of suicide is talking about wanting to die?

If you or someone you know may be at risk for suicide, please call the **National Suicide Prevention Lifeline** at **800-273-8255** night or day. The call is **free** and is **completely confidential**.

To learn more warning signs and how you can help prevent suicide, please visit **www.SuicidePreventionLifeline.org**.

(All profits from the sale of this book will be donated by the author to charities supporting suicide prevention, education and research.)

Read enough? Turn to page 104.

Committing Suicide *for Geniuses*

Did you know that one warning sign of suicide is talking about wanting to die?

If you or someone you know may be at risk for suicide, please call the **National Suicide Prevention Lifeline** at **800-273-8255** night or day. The call is **free** and is **completely confidential.**

To learn more warning signs and how you can help prevent suicide, please visit **www.SuicidePreventionLifeline.org**.

(All profits from the sale of this book will be donated by the author to charities supporting suicide prevention, education and research.)

Read enough? Turn to page 104.

Committing Suicide *for Geniuses*

Did you know that one warning sign of suicide is talking about wanting to die?

If you or someone you know may be at risk for suicide, please call the **National Suicide Prevention Lifeline** at **800-273-8255** night or day. The call is **free** and is **completely confidential**.

To learn more warning signs and how you can help prevent suicide, please visit **www.SuicidePreventionLifeline.org**.

(All profits from the sale of this book will be donated by the author to charities supporting suicide prevention, education and research.)

Read enough? Turn to page 104.

Committing Suicide *for Geniuses*

Did you know that one warning sign of suicide is talking about wanting to die?

If you or someone you know may be at risk for suicide, please call the **National Suicide Prevention Lifeline** at **800-273-8255** night or day. The call is **free** and is **completely confidential**.

To learn more warning signs and how you can help prevent suicide, please visit **www.SuicidePreventionLifeline.org**.

(All profits from the sale of this book will be donated by the author to charities supporting suicide prevention, education and research.)

Read enough? Turn to page 104.

Committing Suicide *for Geniuses*

Did you know that one warning sign of suicide is talking about wanting to die?

If you or someone you know may be at risk for suicide, please call the **National Suicide Prevention Lifeline** at **800-273-8255** night or day. The call is **free** and is **completely confidential**.

To learn more warning signs and how you can help prevent suicide, please visit **www.SuicidePreventionLifeline.org**.

(All profits from the sale of this book will be donated by the author to charities supporting suicide prevention, education and research.)

Read enough? Turn to page 104.

Committing Suicide *for Geniuses*

Committing Suicide *for Geniuses*

Did you know that one warning sign of suicide is talking about wanting to die?

If you or someone you know may be at risk for suicide, please call the **National Suicide Prevention Lifeline** at **800-273-8255** night or day. The call is **free** and is **completely confidential**.

To learn more warning signs and how you can help prevent suicide, please visit **www.SuicidePreventionLifeline.org**.

(All profits from the sale of this book will be donated by the author to charities supporting suicide prevention, education and research.)

Read enough? Turn to page 104.

Committing Suicide *for Geniuses*

Did you know that one warning sign of suicide is talking about wanting to die?

If you or someone you know may be at risk for suicide, please call the **National Suicide Prevention Lifeline** at **800-273-8255** night or day. The call is **free** and is **completely confidential**.

To learn more warning signs and how you can help prevent suicide, please visit **www.SuicidePreventionLifeline.org**.

(All profits from the sale of this book will be donated by the author to charities supporting suicide prevention, education and research.)

Read enough? Turn to page 104.

Committing Suicide *for Geniuses*

Did you know that one warning sign of suicide is talking about wanting to die?

If you or someone you know may be at risk for suicide, please call the **National Suicide Prevention Lifeline** at **800-273-8255** night or day. The call is **free** and is **completely confidential**.

To learn more warning signs and how you can help prevent suicide, please visit **www.SuicidePreventionLifeline.org**.

(All profits from the sale of this book will be donated by the author to charities supporting suicide prevention, education and research.)

Read enough? Turn to page 104.

Did you know that one warning sign of suicide is talking about wanting to die?

If you or someone you know may be at risk for suicide, please call the **National Suicide Prevention Lifeline** at **800-273-8255** night or day. The call is **free** and is **completely confidential**.

To learn more warning signs and how you can help prevent suicide, please visit **www.SuicidePreventionLifeline.org**.

(All profits from the sale of this book will be donated by the author to charities supporting suicide prevention, education and research.)

Read enough? Turn to page 104.

Did you know that one warning sign of suicide is talking about wanting to die?

If you or someone you know may be at risk for suicide, please call the **National Suicide Prevention Lifeline** at **800-273-8255** night or day. The call is **free** and is **completely confidential**.

To learn more warning signs and how you can help prevent suicide, please visit **www.SuicidePreventionLifeline.org**.

(All profits from the sale of this book will be donated by the author to charities supporting suicide prevention, education and research.)

Read enough? Turn to page 104.

Did you know that one warning sign of suicide is talking about wanting to die?

If you or someone you know may be at risk for suicide, please call the **National Suicide Prevention Lifeline** at **800-273-8255** night or day. The call is **free** and is **completely confidential**.

To learn more warning signs and how you can help prevent suicide, please visit **www.SuicidePreventionLifeline.org**.

(All profits from the sale of this book will be donated by the author to charities supporting suicide prevention, education and research.)

Read enough? Turn to page 104.

Did you know that one warning sign of suicide is talking about wanting to die?

If you or someone you know may be at risk for suicide, please call the **National Suicide Prevention Lifeline** at **800-273-8255** night or day. The call is **free** and is **completely confidential**.

To learn more warning signs and how you can help prevent suicide, please visit **www.SuicidePreventionLifeline.org**.

(All profits from the sale of this book will be donated by the author to charities supporting suicide prevention, education and research.)

Read enough? Turn to page 104.

Did you know that one warning sign of suicide is talking about wanting to die?

If you or someone you know may be at risk for suicide, please call the **National Suicide Prevention Lifeline** at **800-273-8255** night or day. The call is **free** and is **completely confidential**.

To learn more warning signs and how you can help prevent suicide, please visit **www.SuicidePreventionLifeline.org**.

(All profits from the sale of this book will be donated by the author to charities supporting suicide prevention, education and research.)

Read enough? Turn to page 104.

Did you know that one warning sign of suicide is talking about wanting to die?

If you or someone you know may be at risk for suicide, please call the **National Suicide Prevention Lifeline** at **800-273-8255** night or day. The call is **free** and is **completely confidential**.

To learn more warning signs and how you can help prevent suicide, please visit **www.SuicidePreventionLifeline.org**.

(All profits from the sale of this book will be donated by the author to charities supporting suicide prevention, education and research.)

Read enough? Turn to page 104.

Committing Suicide *for Geniuses*

Did you know that one warning sign of suicide is talking about wanting to die?

If you or someone you know may be at risk for suicide, please call the **National Suicide Prevention Lifeline** at **800-273-8255** night or day. The call is **free** and is **completely confidential**.

To learn more warning signs and how you can help prevent suicide, please visit **www.SuicidePreventionLifeline.org**.

(All profits from the sale of this book will be donated by the author to charities supporting suicide prevention, education and research.)

Read enough? Turn to page 104.

Committing Suicide *for Geniuses*

Committing Suicide *for Geniuses*

Did you know that one warning sign of suicide is talking about wanting to die?

If you or someone you know may be at risk for suicide, please call the **National Suicide Prevention Lifeline** at **800-273-8255** night or day. The call is **free** and is **completely confidential**.

To learn more warning signs and how you can help prevent suicide, please visit **www.SuicidePreventionLifeline.org**.

(All profits from the sale of this book will be donated by the author to charities supporting suicide prevention, education and research.)

Read enough? Turn to page 104.

Committing Suicide *for Geniuses*

Did you know that one warning sign of suicide is talking about wanting to die?

If you or someone you know may be at risk for suicide, please call the **National Suicide Prevention Lifeline** at **800-273-8255** night or day. The call is **free** and is **completely confidential**.

To learn more warning signs and how you can help prevent suicide, please visit **www.SuicidePreventionLifeline.org**.

(All profits from the sale of this book will be donated by the author to charities supporting suicide prevention, education and research.)

Read enough? Turn to page 104.

Committing Suicide *for Geniuses*

Did you know that one warning sign of suicide is talking about wanting to die?

If you or someone you know may be at risk for suicide, please call the **National Suicide Prevention Lifeline** at **800-273-8255** night or day. The call is **free** and is **completely confidential**.

To learn more warning signs and how you can help prevent suicide, please visit **www.SuicidePreventionLifeline.org**.

(All profits from the sale of this book will be donated by the author to charities supporting suicide prevention, education and research.)

Read enough? Turn to page 104.

Did you know that one warning sign of suicide is talking about wanting to die?

If you or someone you know may be at risk for suicide, please call the **National Suicide Prevention Lifeline** at **800-273-8255** night or day. The call is **free** and is **completely confidential**.

To learn more warning signs and how you can help prevent suicide, please visit **www.SuicidePreventionLifeline.org**.

(All profits from the sale of this book will be donated by the author to charities supporting suicide prevention, education and research.)

Read enough? Turn to page 104.

Committing Suicide *for Geniuses*

Did you know that one warning sign of suicide is talking about wanting to die?

If you or someone you know may be at risk for suicide, please call the **National Suicide Prevention Lifeline** at **800-273-8255** night or day. The call is **free** and is **completely confidential.**

To learn more warning signs and how you can help prevent suicide, please visit **www.SuicidePreventionLifeline.org**.

(All profits from the sale of this book will be donated by the author to charities supporting suicide prevention, education and research.)

Read enough? Turn to page 104.

Committing Suicide *for Geniuses*

Committing Suicide *for Geniuses*

Did you know that one warning sign of suicide is talking about wanting to die?

If you or someone you know may be at risk for suicide, please call the **National Suicide Prevention Lifeline** at **800-273-8255** night or day. The call is **free** and is **completely confidential**.

To learn more warning signs and how you can help prevent suicide, please visit **www.SuicidePreventionLifeline.org**.

(All profits from the sale of this book will be donated by the author to charities supporting suicide prevention, education and research.)

Read enough? Turn to page 104.

Did you know that one warning sign of suicide is talking about wanting to die?

If you or someone you know may be at risk for suicide, please call the **National Suicide Prevention Lifeline** at **800-273-8255** night or day. The call is **free** and is **completely confidential**.

To learn more warning signs and how you can help prevent suicide, please visit **www.SuicidePreventionLifeline.org**.

(All profits from the sale of this book will be donated by the author to charities supporting suicide prevention, education and research.)

Read enough? Turn to page 104.

Did you know that one warning sign of suicide is talking about wanting to die?

If you or someone you know may be at risk for suicide, please call the **National Suicide Prevention Lifeline** at **800-273-8255** night or day. The call is **free** and is **completely confidential**.

To learn more warning signs and how you can help prevent suicide, please visit **www.SuicidePreventionLifeline.org**.

(All profits from the sale of this book will be donated by the author to charities supporting suicide prevention, education and research.)

Read enough? Turn to page 104.

Did you know that one warning sign of suicide is talking about wanting to die?

If you or someone you know may be at risk for suicide, please call the **National Suicide Prevention Lifeline** at **800-273-8255** night or day. The call is **free** and is **completely confidential**.

To learn more warning signs and how you can help prevent suicide, please visit **www.SuicidePreventionLifeline.org**.

(All profits from the sale of this book will be donated by the author to charities supporting suicide prevention, education and research.)

Read enough? Turn to page 104.

Committing Suicide *for Geniuses*

Did you know that one warning sign of suicide is talking about wanting to die?

If you or someone you know may be at risk for suicide, please call the **National Suicide Prevention Lifeline** at **800-273-8255** night or day. The call is **free** and is **completely confidential**.

To learn more warning signs and how you can help prevent suicide, please visit **www.SuicidePreventionLifeline.org**.

(All profits from the sale of this book will be donated by the author to charities supporting suicide prevention, education and research.)

Read enough? Turn to page 104.

Committing Suicide *for Geniuses*

Committing Suicide *for Geniuses*

Did you know that one warning sign of suicide is talking about wanting to die?

If you or someone you know may be at risk for suicide, please call the **National Suicide Prevention Lifeline** at **800-273-8255** night or day. The call is **free** and is **completely confidential.**

To learn more warning signs and how you can help prevent suicide, please visit **www.SuicidePreventionLifeline.org**.

(All profits from the sale of this book will be donated by the author to charities supporting suicide prevention, education and research.)

Read enough? Turn to page 104.

Committing Suicide *for Geniuses*

Did you know that one warning sign of suicide is talking about wanting to die?

If you or someone you know may be at risk for suicide, please call the **National Suicide Prevention Lifeline** at **800-273-8255** night or day. The call is **free** and is **completely confidential**.

To learn more warning signs and how you can help prevent suicide, please visit **www.SuicidePreventionLifeline.org**.

(All profits from the sale of this book will be donated by the author to charities supporting suicide prevention, education and research.)

Read enough? Turn to page 104.

Committing Suicide *for Geniuses*

Did you know that one warning sign of suicide is talking about wanting to die?

If you or someone you know may be at risk for suicide, please call the **National Suicide Prevention Lifeline** at **800-273-8255** night or day. The call is **free** and is **completely confidential**.

To learn more warning signs and how you can help prevent suicide, please visit **www.SuicidePreventionLifeline.org**.

(All profits from the sale of this book will be donated by the author to charities supporting suicide prevention, education and research.)

Read enough? Turn to page 104.

Committing Suicide *for Geniuses*

Did you know that one warning sign of suicide is talking about wanting to die?

If you or someone you know may be at risk for suicide, please call the **National Suicide Prevention Lifeline** at **800-273-8255** night or day. The call is **free** and is **completely confidential**.

To learn more warning signs and how you can help prevent suicide, please visit **www.SuicidePreventionLifeline.org**.

(All profits from the sale of this book will be donated by the author to charities supporting suicide prevention, education and research.)

Read enough? Turn to page 104.

Yep, that's it. That's the whole book.

Honestly, how many more times do we need to repeat it? If fifty times is not enough, we suggest you read the book again. As many times as it takes.

You got the point right away? That's great news, but not surprising. After all… you are a Genius.

 Use it as a notebook. (The left sided pages have been lined for your convenience.)

 "Gift it forward" Give the book to an unsuspecting friend, family member, or colleague—and help raise awareness for suicide prevention, education, and research.

 Add it to your *Just for Geniuses*™ collection. No promises, but serious collectors are expecting the value of all *Just for Geniuses*™ branded merchandise to substantially rise in the decades and centuries ahead.

Nonetheless, we would like to thank you for taking the time to read this book.

We couldn't write books like this without readers like you to support us. Any feedback you give would be greatly appreciated.

Please give us feedback at
www.justforgeniuses.com/feedback

Sorry to hear that. But don't despair. The real power of the *Just for Geniuses*™ brand is the flexibility and the ability to customize it **to your needs**. Think gifts, collectibles, promos, charity fund-raising, corporate events, advocacy, and much more.

Depending on your needs, we have the perfect solution for you:

- Submit a customization request to our design team at no cost. (We will try to accommodate everyone's request based on our discretion.)
- Ask our Professional Services team to assist you (minimum order applies.) This is necessary for time-sensitive requests.
- License *Just for Geniuses*™ for your product, service, or media needs. This would give you the most flexibility.

What are you waiting for? Submit your request today at **www.justforgeniuses.com/solutions**

Committing Suicide *for Geniuses*

www.justforgeniuses.com

www.ingramcontent.com/pod-product-compliance
Lightning Source LLC
Chambersburg PA
CBHW070853050426
42453CB00012B/2186